Here in There

Here in There

Angela Carr

BookThug · 2014

The production of this book was made possible through the generous assistance
of the Canada Council for the Arts and the Ontario Arts Council.

LIBRARY AND ARCHIVES CANADA CATALOGUING IN PUBLICATION

Carr, Angela, 1976–, author
    Here in there / Angela Carr.

Poems.
Issued in print and electronic formats.
ISBN 978-1-77166-032-7 (PBK.). – ISBN 978-1-77166-041-9 (PDF)

    I. Title.

PS8605.A7728H47 2014   C811'.6   C2013-908729-X
                                           C2013-908730-3

PRINTED IN CANADA

Table of Contents

Signs of Interest

Iris gave her attention to the news. Iris gave her attention to relatives on the telephone. Iris gave her attention to writing letters. Iris gave her attention to protests. Iris gave her attention to the institution. Iris gave her letters to officials. Iris gave her time to relatives. Iris gave her letters to institutions. At last the storm was passing. Iris was late according to her relatives. The meal was nearly over. The car was damaged. Her experience was documented in a letter that described the future passing over her, beyond reach. There was no ceiling within sight. Interest was floating over her. It was another name for time. The herd is numberless. Since to whisper is grammar. It is a description of time. It underwrites everything. It is simple and declarative. It is red and digital. It is the emptying of contingency – an escape. Iris gave herself to laughter. Iris gave herself to rejecting the apparatus while fantasizing about convent life. Iris characterized the nation's sudden and unified decision to vote differently as a residual Catholic tendency. The unrecognized nation within a larger, recognized nation had voted for an unknown, socialist, federal party. The unrecognized nation voted cynically and in unison and formed the official opposition within the recognized nation.

I gave my attention to the pause. I gave my attention to the frozen Skype image. I gave my attention to waiting. We were on hold. We could see but not touch and yet touch was composing us. We were broken only where skin could not answer. Iris' skin is ornamented with tattooed threads, mingling with each other in scrolls and coils, and alternating with straight lines. An image is truly raw and visible, fibres and sinews, strips and straps. The sense of beauty merges with and is consumed by the sense of reminiscence. Iris shuts down her computer. Iris stands up. Iris stretches her neck, shoulders, back. Iris shakes the cramps from her elbows, wrists. Iris releases, recollects.

I was directed away from the Everywhere Beautiful. I turned off my computer. I stood up. I stretched. I entered the kitchen. I gave my attention to the refrigerator. I sought its answers. I sought the composition of preservation in the cramped space of provisions. I sought the composition of attention. I gave my attention to an avocado. I gave my attention to a knife. I gave my attention to olive oil, salt, lemon. I cut slowly and meticulously, a soft human hand with its tools. I enhanced the details. Often I could recall nothing but our shared question. Its recurring figure was our uncertain future.

Iris gave her attention to the slow sun of the afternoon. Iris gave her attention to the vicious conflict. Iris gave her attention to the rule of one. Iris gave her attention to the silence of deliberation. Iris gave her attention to the signature on the paper. Iris gave her attention to the pen. Iris gave her attention to the yellow hue of the legal document. Iris gave herself a moment in which she could reflect. Iris found calm in this evaluation. Iris found silence in this calmness. Iris gave her attention to the shadow on the X-ray. Iris gave her attention to the calendar on the physician's wall.

Iris gave her attention to the calm of the signature. Iris gave her attention to the disinfected surface of a counter. Iris signed a cheque. Iris gave her attention to a stethoscope. Iris gave her attention to a white sheet of paper pulled over the examining table. Iris gave her attention to green lawns. Iris gave her attention to the herbicidal regularity of grass. Iris gave her attention to the brightness of the afternoon. Iris gave her attention to the invisible toxicity of the suburb. Iris gave her attention to the visible toxicity of the city. Iris folded the pollution of desire with care. Iris gave her attention to the fold. Iris folded the attention of brightness, of the X-ray. Iris folded the attention of visibility.

Iris unwound her scarf. Iris asked a question of an attendant. Iris waited in line. Iris saw smiling passengers. Iris saw well-dressed passengers. Iris chose a seat. Iris searched her bag. Iris misplaced a device. Iris closed her eyes. Iris pressed her head back. Iris stood up. Iris walked to the back of the bus. Iris sat down. Iris discreetly brushed away a teardrop. Iris picked up her bag with brevity. Iris entered the story. Iris unwound her scrutiny. Iris asked a question of the organizer. Iris waited in line. Iris saw smiling passengers. Iris saw well-dressed passengers. Iris chose the wrong seat. Iris listened to deliberations. Iris closed her eyes. Iris saw red on black. Iris evaluated and labelled her options. Iris made pencil checks in boxes. Iris took a sip of coffee. Iris listened to deliberations. Iris wished the teardrops could flow freely. Iris chose to remain silent.

Iris desired silence. Iris' desire searched.

Iris walked away from the interrogation desk. Iris reboarded the bus. Iris gave her attention to the regularity of upholstery on the ceiling and chairs. Iris gave her attention to the dominance of upholstery. Iris gave her attention to the relative invisibility of patterns. Iris gave her attention to the detail of a voice and a signature. Iris gave her attention to the visibility of the irregular. We shifted our bags and shrugged off our coats. We attended to our travel documents carefully. We were re-emerging as individuals from persons with spatial origins. I gave my attention to the purse at my foot and to my leg stretched awkwardly into the aisle. I gave my attention to the volume of chatter, to untangling languages. I gave my attention to the coat folded under my head and to the pinched circulation in my leg. I gave my attention to the smell of nail polish, of varnish. I gave my attention to the toxicity of full, inelastic and completely rigid forms. I heard the elevation of activity to durability. I heard canons forming from important consequences. I heard great upper structures supported by terraces. I heard intermediary figures moored at the bottom of thought, retaining meaning reductively and symbolically. I heard supporting parts of words, shadows and letters. I followed their indications. I heard an almost exclusively mechanical technique and a less frequent offering of poetry. I heard elements of *bottom, least, superficial,* of *profundity, terra* and *truth.* I heard truth in the word varnish. I heard the greater detail of the place name tear the fabric of language. I saw us through the gap created by the place name. I chose to tear through the textile with the nail of that name.

We heard truth in the word, tearing. Banknotes, flags and passports could be torn but the hard material of coins, screens and credit cards could not. We followed glass, a material that cannot be torn, to its beginning with geometry. We secured rectangular windows versus the complexity of leaves, which can be torn. We heard the end of the poetic line as it turns relentlessly, whether cutting, breaking or tearing. We read *The Ear of the Other*. In any case the proper name is the only thing that does not change in translation, said Jacques Derrida. Even numbers may change. We read an essay by Norma Cole about Samuel Beckett who turns the ten nights of *Le Bateau Ivre* into nine.

We heard *green* tear in the word, ephemeral. Vertebrae of spring cast their shadows on the place name. We can follow this spine where the flesh of the greater body is ephemeral. We can follow the ephemeral and describe it from a point of view created by the place name. There is no more pattern in any torn fabrication. We can follow the hoax, be taken in, swindled. To be green, to be gullible, to be young. I heard the subway passing beneath the building six stories below. I heard the insistence of near and distant memories. Interest shuttled past rapidly. I gave my attention to credit. I inscribed my signature on the screen with a bare finger. I credited my senses with the accumulation of fluctuating reflections. Released cellularly, memory is sensuous, more exaggerated and raw.

I gave my attention to participating as a spectator. Credit erected a temporary structure over memory.

Iris leapt risky lengths joyously and fell into dereliction. This was her pattern. We descended into credit. We feigned communities of ownership and compared our names within the false safety of collectivity. We were the minions of solidarity or we were the champions of solidarity. We were compact, balmy, atlases. An enduring crowd of desire. Iris gave her attention to the nation. A hard surface is forever worn by a fluid surface that has no form. Iris gave her attention to the country. The country was not more or less abrasive than the nation, nor was it more or less abraded. Iris described the nation as a feeling of ritualized familial pressure. A vibrational fluid state with no visible imprint, however disputatious like the law. I read *metabolism, intellectual, depression.*

The descriptive function was monophonic and joints in the city's water pipes were made of lead. Iris described the coat of arms that belonged to her atrophying family. It was ornamental but void in the centre. Across a vacant middle ground, swords majestically raised and a lion's head emphatically repeated. Ribbons, sharp points of blade ends, a curling yellow frame, a billowing leaf, the first three letters of atheism, a splinter of wood, ether, a glazed roof, a support, a cavity, an allergen, an email, holding up the heavens, cruelty, extremity, exclusion. Oh coastguard, oh snowcock.

Here begins as I am questioning its softness. Here children are sleeping. Here, citizens, asleep. Here is inhabited the relief of home. Here brocades resilient surfaces of sleep. Here the tireless border guards. Here the nation is a fog that does not disperse by mid-day. Here labour invokes the focus of attention. Here is the intention of wooden furniture in a forest. A production of semblance. Poetry, distillation, desire. I have invited you here. Here is the way attention folds on itself. Light indisposed to beauty. Iris is a messenger in these lines cast here without characters. We are not our names but the residue of advantage there perceived as disadvantage.

The library ceiling was aqua and gold. Iris waited for a rare book to be brought out from a closed stack. Iris gave her attention to surprising 19th-century colour prints. Iris gave her attention to symmetry. Symmetry was a factor of excessive influence, a flat weaving of desire. Symmetry bides its time for a perfect illusion. Yet the act of waiting has no parallel: it is an instance of asymmetry. Iris gave her attention to the singularity of a unique action. A bias is a systematic distortion in the social fabric. Ambition is a determination, an upward measure. Iris gave her attention to the century. Let's compile an index of its errors. Iris gave her attention to suppleness. Not truth but the fact of weather without borders. Here, pages were cracking. Water creaked through the pipes in the building. There were 156 units. Every amatory relation contained within the urban ambit both vast and minuscule. Iris and I were the creation of parts of an amorous whole or a composite beast that could express nothing more frightening than love's unrelenting desire for beauty. Whether in the symmetry of agreement or in symmetry of judgment, we were blushing.

Currency

When I board the train ahead of Iris, I choose the only windowless row of seats. When everything enclosed, protected and covered presents itself as unified. Speckled granite-coloured, the dull laminate sheen of the Amtrak wall. Cadences of recurring decorative features. When I open my laptop. When I nearly look. When I nearly sleep. When uniform segments of space bind to form an enclosure. We cannot know exactly what we are leaving. There are no windows by which anything comes in or goes out. There are neither openings nor doorways.

8 AM. Split ends. Dandruff flurry. Iris blow-dries her hair. Forced hot air throws into relief the comb's monotony. I should leave out further details. We can be repeatedly described but never illustrated. We can obtain a more or less relief-like design by naming Iris. The style of this practice is both linear and free. When reliefs appear initially as a secondary surface. When later we see the triviality of any surface. When the more obvious designs are the sum of crossing the border x number of times. When in embroidery and knitted materials, such tendentious monotony of patterning. Symmetrical arrangements of symbols provoke such neutrality. When our covers are unseen and unheard under other covers. Even bright covers are controlled by the manufacturer. When the surface

is raised with the cross-stitch. The border is patrolled but never described. We discover methods for detachment. We should cross at regular intervals. When the pieces of time must be preserved. This stitch. A name. Iris departs.

When Iris lays herself open, the walls are covered not in aristocratic textiles but in paper collage. When a secondary surface, a relief. A tourist in the hallway. When her neighbours listen to each other's organs. When the walls are that thin. They do not withstand the mere imprint of a thumb. When she does not listen to reason, the fire escape forms a zigzag scaffolding. When the walls become a simple refinement lacking description. When she regains her period. When the slut. When the hunger. When the moment. She pays for her deep critique of this system. (With pleasure. *A bacchante, a strumpet of care.*) There is no loop stitch. When the shallow imprint of a thumb. When the thin walls continue to allude to impossible refinement. When differentiation might have isolated moments. When she had little exact knowledge of where she was living. When this *where* was a moment in thinking. Motion was intrinsic to the simple substance. There was no communication. The vessel was floating fathomlessly. It was a subject. Then it was an embodiment of time and place. The law of the moment of which we could have little exact knowledge. It was always before or behind us.

Small lights emerging in a curve along a dark highway. Ephemeral, losing, immoderate. In pointless fog, extinguished. Slipping forward into periphery, focal, astir. Slight and clear. Headlights appearing as inverse asterisks, omitted matter. Night's total assurance signals their fleetingness. Receding. Insistence. Recoiled amber highway lines in the rearview mirror. Taut forgery explicit and empty. The man reading. The woman with. The man working. Great invisible body of this connecting preposition: the highway. Prepositions relating weaponry to containers. Conveying. Small lights approaching as weaponry and receding as containers. Iris lies in bed. Iris lies in connecting matter. Iris lies abundantly. Iris does not rise.

Liquidity

Distorted music to sustain Iris while on hold, interspersed with recurring reminders that she is waiting. Iris feels her life becoming a series of errands. Iris survives by infiltrating impenetrable networks of institutions and corporations. The open is blind to itself and gives itself up too readily. The rabble to which Iris is attracted becomes transparent, the substance of rainstorms. Transient desire exalted to absolute status, soon to be captured, the water of mourning. Some of us experience nostalgia for the passing of our desire before it passes. Some of us are the principled shade of precision and some of us are the serious partition of doubt. In early morning light, the street was precious apparition. Early morning light performed on an anatomy of silence. I was reading Jabès, "The ear is a silence."

Her face: an alchemy of silences. Her voice: an early morning light. It appears to renew the city, which cannot be touched except by light. Lips do yet. On Iris' ear, their motion is heard and held.

Long after the flood has subsided, its motion will be captured and held still in this room. Traces of nostalgia will moisten the cracked epistolary form. A yell from the sidewalk will subside. A surge of violence will subside. Daylight will take a cue from the soothing evening and withdraw. Decaying phosphorescence streaks the sky. We borrow these so-called wasted hours when the labour of spent time ceases. Darkness slides around brilliantly lit billboards. We hazard a misplaced I. We hazard a language of coldness. In early light, when language forged my disparition, I conjured myself as a cue. I appeared in the text where the silence of the ear needed to be qualified as receptive, not passive. I received the text and it registered my reception. In early light, language forged my disappearance.

Language was the reason of my possession. Language was what dispossessed me.

I conjured myself as a cue, a cloud, a beacon, a whisper, a bird call, *une berceuse, une rumeur*. I suppressed my language when we reached the border. We waited in the car under photo radar. We answered questions. We had never had another name. No criminal records. No pardons. No activity whatsoever. I suppressed my feelings. I responded blankly and calmly to sarcasm. The silence of sustainability is furrowed with traces of queer feelings. This performance of our disappearance numbingly well practiced and routine.

Iris pocket-dials me repeatedly along the I-87. She is sleeping on her phone. It is 10 AM, it is 8 AM, it is 11 AM. Structural distortion caused by a frozen binary becomes more pronounced in the nation. Silence gathers around leafless scenery. *Iris refuse le pouvoir de sa solitude.* Yet the silence of sustainability is no action. No action alone is sustainable. Wedged in the interstice between action and doubt, we are never so secure as to think we have abandoned bitterness entirely. We pine for action. We abandon commerce. We choose abandonment over abasement. We do not rise. We refuse to hold out our hands. We refuse to ask. Iris holds back. Iris does not rise. Abandonment is unheard, the motion of an ear. I lay on my back. I turned my head, pressing an ear to the floor. I looked over my left hand, running a finger along the baseboard. I looked into endeavours lost to silence. Hours silenced in faded, yellowing blinds. I jabbed my finger into dust. The time of day rose, a perplexing image. We walked onto the street, letting the heavy door clang shut behind us. The time of day rose inside our cloud of non-interventionist policy. We searched high and low in this dust cloud for our disguise, our disparition, abandoning ourselves head-first in this – replace "hell" with this paradigm. Come this paradigm or high water, long after the flood has subsided, time is reckless, this paradigm bent. It's the contraction of daylight in mid-winter. Iris blames her silence for lost time. Lost time is a spoil to be gained by violence or silence. Iris will not choose violence. This is a turgence in time, swelling at the site of love's reception. I waited for Iris on the cold metal bench. I stood to unsettle the cold from my limbs. Poetry was a flood that had subsided, leaving only its frozen puddles of water between the protruding roots of trees. I waited in opposition to the disjuncture of contemporaneity. We were on hold. On hold we experienced the irrelevance of paroxysm. On hold, we arrived at a disjuncture, not a point.

Other Signs

The first impression a name makes is as a motif,
the talon or claw of an animal.

Its sex is civilized in the bureaucratic form.

The name is easily replaced, or it is the unattainable extreme of any designation.

The name is a property of invention. Imperial, it is indifferent to heat and cold.

The name in its powdered state presents us with an opportunity to share instant refreshments in a waiting room surrounded by magnificent flowers.

The name is a trace of placation in the hierarchy of desires. It slips between choice and another's indication of belonging. A door, any name rotates on the axis of identity.

A lack of name would mean to have no place.

A name is any number of cities. Wind drives its enactment.

A name is any number of exits.

Ornamental letters are created from rows of flat stitching.

The maximum strength of any geometric pattern depends on a balance of tension vectors.

Then I may cease to address you by name.

This name is like the dyed wool of living sheep.

A row is formed first by making the stitches meet,
second by making them touch along their length, partly
or completely.

The names form a chain, back and forth
fasten, tie, tack
they draw attention to the embodiment of patterns.

We formed the borderline between the name and its debt.

The name owed everything to the chain.

Monochrome was the error of economic conception.

The fastening of ecstasy stripped of its colour.

Credit was rapidly forming fresh public opinion.

What is said about glass and its hardness can also be said about currency.

The name is distributed against a monotonous background of vibrating colour.

I could name the exquisite principle that sustains diversity.

This "I" names the level opposition between extremes.

Iris is as much a name as an archive. A situation rightly unaided – velvet.

There were rules with fine vents impervious to representation.

There were remarks as wrong as their identities.

The name was an exception.

Its design, something hanging down,
mediating a contrast between head and ground.

This is the gravity of your name when the sun enters your
constellation.

This is how absolute formal beauty serves every technical purpose.

I was beckoned by the place name into credit.

What we guard is what can be credited to us.

Now the cells are insisting on this process.

*The name of that is of course money, and
the absurd trust in value is the pattern of
bond and contract and interest – just where
the names are exactly equivalent to the trust
given to them.* – J.H. Prynne

First Signs

Just after a layer of dark cloud, there's a break in the silence,
a dog barking overheard through the woods
close to Route 6

Just after the two sisters have unfurled their kites and established
    that one string
is markedly longer so long in fact the kite would fly above the
    cloud if unwound
Just after the two sisters have disputed and confirmed the relative
    reach of their kites

Just after we arrive via our downward trek to the beach
and the relative status of our kites high and low
$7.99 for this kite, $23.99 for that

Just after the phone does not ring and no one writes
Just after the paint peels from the walls
Just after the walls peel from the posts
and the bed is standing alone in a field of lilacs

Just after the fantastic has succeeded in following every accident
    to the real

Just after: before the "long after" described by Rimbaud
Just after the Paris Commune of 1871 is defeated by Versailles
which is more like "well after" or "certainly after," "after a certain
    time"

After a time there is this word peeling from that field
and there is my vocabulary peeling from its debt, our feelings
    from my memory

Just after I wrote: overheard a dog, I wanted to add, *But can one
    overhear a dog?*
To overhear is to hear something one is not privy to

If I own no private land, what am I privy to?
Or is this poem private?
What is its status? Is it high or low?

Just after every cracked structure becomes something we are privy to
and just after overhearing
becomes a form of misplaced
hearing

Just after I wrote: a form of, I wanted to add, *What shape is that?*
This was a crack in the language of Québec that I am privy to, so
   to speak

Just after the industry of robins at the window and beyond the
   screen door's softness
Just after triangular branching repeats an idea of rough origins its
   delicate naming
Just after the naming of this cracked structure peels from what we
   are privy to,
asymptotic and manifest

Just after: And what does it mean to write an occasional poem?
And what does it mean to have the privilege of distance from
    which to reflect and write?
The privilege of distance from which to overhear?

To be privileged to a language
that is the language of a nation
as though one were apart:
this crack in my respect is a dangerous becoming that I am
    privy to in order to speak

I must or the real translates my respect as a form of apartness

I must, in a ritual sense: the grammar of music

If I begin again, it's because money has its local specificity

At first we weighed money and then we only needed to see money
    to determine its value

We saw money alone and we saw money connecting needs

We saw the noun of money form from the connecting *and*
that was the first noun
just after we saw it separately

Just after the mayor forbids protests in his city and *soucis* sprout
through the civic cracks

Worries are cellular and solicitous: incited by the demands
of legal insistence,
worries wedged between names
and debts

After a time we see only the first signs: squares
and rectangles stamped with bars of hard metal
onto soft drops of precious metal.

Acknowledgements

Parts of this book were previously published in *Lana Turner: A Journal of Poetry and Opinion* (Cal Bedient and David Lau), *The Volta* (Joshua Marie Wilkinson), *Canada and Beyond: A Journal of Canadian Literary and Cultural Studies* (Erín Moure), *New American Writing* (Maxine Chernoff and Paul Hoover) and in a chapbook called *Hedges* (Bronwyn Haslam). Thanks to the editors.

Writing this book, I was sustained by the conversation and generosity of my friends. Special thanks to Kyra Revenko, Marc Guastavino, Erín Moure, Lisa Robertson, Bronwyn Haslam, Eric Savoy, Chantal Neveu, and Rachel Levitsky for being there. To Jay and Hazel Millar of BookThug, thank you for your unwavering belief in me. Thanks to Isidora and Neve for bright and lively company. For necessary enthusiasm, steadfast encouragement and editorial acuity, love and thanks to Kate Eichhorn.

About the Author

Angela Carr is the author of the poetry books, *Ropewalk* (2006; nominated for the McAuslan First Book Prize) and *The Rose Concordance* (2009). In addition, she translated *Coït* by Chantal Neveu (2012). Originally from Montréal, Carr now lives in New York City, where she teaches creative writing at the New School for Liberal Arts.

Colophon

Manufactured as the first edition of *Here in There* in the spring of
2014 by BookThug. Distributed in Canada by the Literary Press
Group www.lpg.ca. Distributed in the United States by Small Press
Distribution www.spdbooks.org. Shop online at www.bookthug.ca

BOOK
PRODUCTION
WAR ECONOMY
STANDARD

Type + design: Jay MillAr
Copy edited by Ruth Zuchter